MW01687018

In a country whose name keeps changing, a woman longs to return to an imaginary past. Part fiction, part biography, part fairy-tale, *Weave* is a photograph that fell onto the rails when the story-teller changed trains. Or perhaps it slipped into the waves of the lake when her two-seater plane took off. Or she tore it into pieces and buried it in the woods, to keep it safe. Now she's searching for her lost identity, from the banks of the Danube, to the port of Istanbul, to the frozen edge of Lake Ontario. She's looking for some fragment of home to give meaning to her pile of passports, left like ghosts in the bottom of a drawer.

Acknowledgements

Some of these poems previously appeared in the 2003 Salt Press anthology *100 Poets Against the War* and the literary magazines *Exile*, *Pharos*, and *Upstairs at Duroc*.

Merci Ellis Avery, Barbara Beck, Lauren B. Davis, Jennifer K.Dick, Ethan Gilsdorf, Michelle Noteboom and Todd Swift for their help in developing these poems. Thank you to Bremner Duthie & my family for their love and support.

Contents

Weave

What begins begins now. it is here, the we which is beginning
begins
now and no turning from it, there will be only this beginning and
no turning back even as we, she,
move forward further, far further away

from her, this, ours, which begins. what begins

begins here.

my life has not gone by the book. according to plan, I mean
which book?

a romantic novelist (is there any other) dreams himself away to Prague during the long Toronto winter. he is waiting for Lake Ontario to freeze so he might walk across the ice into my voice, this accent of mine denting pronunciation, whatever the language.

you'll never guess where I'm from.

a map, take a pushpin (Pushkin), a thumbtack to pin down that country whose name keeps changing

I changed my own name once too. shortened myself, cut off six names and never heard them again. no loss. just an invitation to schizophrenia

to give a girl seven first names. all seven of her aunts. I decided on just one. the shortest.

then there is a gap

—ah that blank, the sudden gap of certain years, a war particular to the past century or so you tell yourselves, skirting around the obvious repetitions.

my brother spent this blank space in an emptiness he does not discuss, simply emerging on the other side, thinly.
I have never asked.
a respect for

silence and
music and
books, it is meet to respect only these. in this
I suppose I could be Viennese after all.

I must tell you of the house in Vienna.

hum the Blue Danube

1.

there was a house on the canal in Vienna, in the middle of the city,
on the canal, there was a house, a restaurant, a shop in which to
buy candy. there was the waltz, the opera, the theatre. burned
by the russians, burned, I would like to blame everything on the
russians, excepting the candyshop and Mr. Spitzer and Mrs.
Spitzer. who disappeared before. the shop
went empty, that yellow paper in the corner of its window.
everything can be blamed on someone. Mr. Spitzer's goatee.
he would give always our choice of candy when we left town
again, a train ride, for our hour's trip on the train
to Asch home again home again sucking the candy from the
Spitzer's candyshop. which is gone, which has been gone since,
and anyhow
the building was burned to the ground by the russians, there is
only a parking lot there now.
by the canal, by the Danube in Vienna, there is only a lot
in which to park cars. there is no house.

2.

strange to visit the spa that spring. everyone spoke german, all the
tourists once so international, all their languages turned
to german. the men in their black velour hats, they had
disappeared already. I did not know then what absence means.
the town was so sober and tidy, but
I had sprained my ankle hiking in the Erzgebirge forest and
couldn't dance anyhow.

3.

the initials I kept, I chose
(for there were too many when I married)
the silverware had my initials HMH. this silver we gave to the
secretary of a civil servant in Prague, a friend. then
in '44 they left for south america somewhere there is
my silver I imagine they sold it piece by piece, my initials set out
on a table in
Buenos Aires or Montevideo.

4.

they might still tell this story, those two boys.
replanting the willow trees outside my window they
came upon two square gin bottles, one full, you never know
when that might be useful, and the other, emptied of liquor, I
long ago
refilled with hundred dollar bills, U.S.
I think the boys had never seen those before.
my husband took the two bottles and nodded and did not explain
to these two teenagers hired for the gardening. what would they
understand of it, born so
secure beside this lake. they have no idea and why
should we be the ones to enlighten them.

let us step around this time

take my arms, we might dance
do you know how to tango? or maybe some kind
of two-step, we could learn
the Charleston.

this is a story from world war I it is
a story for which there is no witness, for I wasn't born or even
thought of. I was only told about this war
by my elder brother and then he died. in this story, it is still 1917.
he is tall and almost-blond and no one expects him yet, us yet,
to disappear

so for this first war, when I am not yet born,
there is a story about uniforms. the cloth needed by the army
new recruits are always but always
given freshly-made fatigues, let them go cleanly, someone
thought it an honest cliché.

there's a lot of cloth needed in wartime. a war is good for business
when you're in textiles

after a while the shortages set in. this is the real beginning of most
war stories.

they began sending us uniforms
taken from the dead. any denomination of man.
a body's not worth a soldier's cloth. you know
how they died in that war, don't you? the shortest
english word is mud. what they turned into.

railway cars piled with uniforms arrived at our factory. my brother
eric's job it was to cut off the buttons, medals, any metal clasps
or zippers,
anything that wasn't cloth

take the remaining fabric, soak it, vats full in the factory,
break down the fibres
reweave it into new cloth, fresh. ready. my elder brother eric
only wondering

right at the end whether these uniforms were coming through
repeatedly, unending, his hands going over the cloth, the buttons,
the dead men.
he would wash his hands. he was only thirteen and he had buttons
from all over the world, he was proud of his war metal collection.

it included colours from every country.
you understand what I mean. the dead
came from everywhere.

we three

there were three generations in the house

it was a big yellow house in a country whose name keeps changing

the remarkable structure of the matriarch, her gold hair and rigid
posture. now I know it was all done with whalebone.

we lived beneath the reign of whale bones:
three adults and their five children.

the five children, begin with eric my brother, my elder, my long-
dead perfect brother. then in order of age, my two irrelevant
cousins,
their names have never been
important, followed next by me, the long-lived flaw,
and then there was Wilhelm,
the youngest of us, my brother Wilhelm who even tiny was
my ally, my alloy—we were the perfect mixture of two metals.

we should have known we were inseparable,
that whatever happened we would
come back to each other.

there isn't any
one you can trust apart from yourself, I know that, but
between Wilhelm and I there was
a constant exception.

it was always understood
between us, and my husband, ever after—how can I say this
accurately
or with fairness?—sometimes
I think he wished
that it was Wilhelm he had married,
not me.

central europe not
eastern

look at a map

the Republic as fairy tale

imagine
this is a story beginning
in the fourteenth century, in the woods

the rolled crumbs
of bread have been eaten
by squirrels or rats, depending
on much you want to frighten
your children as you tell them the story

there are details Grimm omitted
to give him a poet's license: such details
do not always make the story better in its telling, retelling

so you don't know the miller's name was Hans
that his children whom he loved
were difficult and strange, and sometimes
he thought his first wife
must truly have been a gypsy, for Hansel and Gretel's dark eyes
saw best at the light of the moon; he remembers
his first wife dancing, it is what she did best

let us be blunt: she left. and later in the fairy tale, who is
that witch in the woods? the question
must be asked. that witch, her black eyes, surely she is
their real mother, who disappeared. and Hans, who did not
go after her? men are sometimes such innocents

stepmothers were as common in 1341 as they are
now. they do their best, even here in Bohemia,
where anything can happen, and has.
where the inhabitants of these towns proudly show
their conservative colours, their passion for industry. they resent
Puccini's *Bohème*, they disapprove
of magic. it is false advertising.

Bohemia
is not where you think. there are gypsies, yes, ask Hans, he'll look away and think
about his children, how in Prague
gypsies are beaten, their apartments burned

but we

were in the woods, with Hansel and Gretel, rolling
crumbs into pebbles and placing them
along the path

so we won't get lost in all this history

to follow the true story through
to the witch's house and beyond

let me hand you a picture:

this is Wilhelm & me,

we have always
travelled together, I as the tomboy & he
delicate, fragile — the boy as teacup, made only
of the thinnest porcelain. and I
made of mud.

our parents were vehement tourists. my mother might
evince a sudden
interest in Alexandria & suddenly we were setting out for Egypt
all equipped,
tutors in tow,
our father beside an Egyptian businessman, discussing
industrial dyeing machines, barely
nodding at the pyramids

while my mother dressed us in safari ensembles, all of us out
to see the world via amusements in Monte Carlo

Wilhelm poisoned himself with whiskey; I was bitten
by a camel, we were
bitten by a desire
to never go home. we didn't know there would be a time
when home
was impossible. it is one thing to leave
your parents' house. another to say, looking back over your
shoulder,
it is not the body
that is turned to salt.

favourite

the player pianos
picked out their silken tune, their cotton rhythm

our bloodlines paced according to that shuttle

what pattern I'd make of that cloth. folded and folded and folded

a place above the factory drying rooms,
conjunction of two eaves, climbing up
along the gutter careful about my dress. any mark betrays

the building used to breathe, a great well-oiled animal
kept us enmeshed, threaded through our landscape

draw a line from this old kitchen
knedliky

they are cooking plums, the kitchen is
entirely plum. I stand on the lintel
arms outstretched balance in the doorway. plum plum I say to
myself

they will be dumpling or they will be jam

I have always been partial to dumplings,
to strict family recipe.

I have always been somewhat inclined to resemble
a dumpling,

just settled in gravy, a stick to your ribs-ness
it's what you are brought up with that is comforting.
in China we ate congee,
I recognized that stick-to-it-ness

Bohemia and Canton both
living off pork, dough, some few sticky things

geography (the Coasts of Bohemia)

I was twelve when I learned of Shakespeare.
I was not ignorant. And you, when did you first hear
of Goethe? of Strauss?

let's talk about Kafka. tell me, why
is he called a german writer
when it is Prague, the city which befits him?

but. I was talking of Shakespeare, who gave the landscape
where I was born elaborate coasts, waters and sand.

for the sake of clarity, I would like to say: there are
no deserts in the place that was I born. there is
no sea which licks those lands. no ship can touch upon our shores
unless Poland sink or all of germany disappear.
upon our shores in fact is all of europe.

whatever colour the lines
on the map, Prague is there in the middle
where the heart should be.

there is no explanation suitable for a girl of thirteen burdened by intellect

yet
in the private
racetrack of her mind,
where everyone dressed as for Ascot,
she took up occupations as other girls might
imagine marriage. she invented herself archeologist
or sailor—disguised as a boy of course, though occasionally,
spitefully
after another irritating dress fitting, all right, she will envisage
herself as courtesan, influential in Paris & Vienna, holding
passionate intellectual court. then staring into the mirror how
sadly impossible, frowning at her face too round. her mother said
she looked
like a peasant. curse the diets she foresaw in her future. the slow
walk downstairs to ask the cook for a bowl of cherries, to eat
one by one by one, arranging the pits in piles of three on white
tablecloth in rows like soldiers.

the factory

what will or will not be good for the
company. father and the brothers meeting and not

the daughter or the mother, never at meetings for
factory or company. family's business, what will be good for.

whose family then, whose business then. I can do books, though
not trained.

what was it, I was to keep my mind occupied? idle hands,
something about the devil?

always there was a body underneath

laughing

the Industrialist

a stereotype I was unaware of until I moved to england.
but allow me to pause, allow me this pleasure
of explanation:

you see, I grew up a believer.

industry wasn't mere industriousness. it was
the village all around, it was
the purpose for everything, it was
source of father's car and of
my governess's new boots and of mother's disinterested trips.

it was a more than merely the simple buying of things. no,
it was an entire, a complicated,
system of belief, I explain this badly, I mean
the cotton threads, their spin—

listen to the machinery, weaving itself into
bloomers and knickers and inelegant
useful apparel that keeps a person warm against damp and cold,
this same cotton thread that came into our factory,
that came from India, from Egypt,
the wool from sheep right there, over some hills, I searched the
atlas to find the thread
that came into Asch, through Fleissen. the thread which became
underclothes
in our factory.
bought by women in britain and germany and russia. moving
through the world, from a warmer place to a colder one

shillings, pfennigs, roubles, would roll
slowly on their wheeled edges back
to our tiny town in
the Republic, with these coins the butcher, the candlestick maker,
the whole of us would have money to spend

all due to this cotton thread. it spread a sort of web across the continent, it made roads
out of the map of the world, I pictured our continent woven neatly through with cotton thread

you could say it was the factory's machinery
that held what I knew of the world together.

tangerine

what is a nationality anyhow but a bit of paper proving your
worth. there is no point in discussing that country, I would not
know
what to call it now

gypsies. from the word Egyptian, yes Egypt is the place
the british thought the Rom came from. believing Bohemia
must be right nearby. for this
I will cite Sir Walter Scott, for his words
are as good as any

> *"I am whatever the Europeans may choose to call me;*
> *but I have no country"*

have no country.

it is most irritating that I don't have access to my books.
my citations must
needs be rough. let me see,

> *"a quarrelling people" "in a faraway country"*
> *"of whom we know nothing"*

who knows what of nothing? I used to fantasize
that I would take a ship from Montreal along the St. Lawrence,
across the Atlantic, yes return to the Continent and on a train
roll all the way back to Prague, to see what had become
of a particular
pastry shop

but to be there even in memory requires
such balance and stealth, swimming down

exhale

which part isn't the one you want?

it seems a long time ago, when my husband made three

we married in a rush, he was sent back after two weeks.
they were in france by then. he left me a painting of the alps.

you want I should explain love like a cake? I cut that cake
into pieces,
one for each of my stale loyalties. I have worn the prettiest
expectations for people like you.

as for love, haven't you learned that lesson yet? everything
coexists. three is a better number than two, it is more believable.

let me give you an example. something impossible. what if you
disappeared for three years; who would you find in your house
when you returned?

would she invite you in? would she lend you clean clothes?
would she give you her clean hands. or send you out ahead of her

kiss you once and push you forward through the woods. would
the cake
in your pocket crumble, its pieces now dry?

I married for love

and though today I might mock such a sentiment

it is there none the less, these things do not sift away (no real emotion is sand)

I was never a wide-eyed youth or a pretty girl, I was only impressed

he was good at what he did. I admired that. he was clear-eyed and the blue sky complemented him.

I will say at least that I think I was happy. I didn't smile and I had no stockings to be married in but I think I was happy. Wilhelm handed me away

in two weeks I was back at my grandmother's house, keeping the factory books

while the men turned into green mysteries two at a time

Wilhelm sent north and then no word at all except they think

(it was my husband only who dissented:
    it's a clear thing, you would know if he died. it means he's not dead. you would know it)

iron cross

I would say lightly that he made of his options a noble choice, but really
there is rarely more than one option:

the best way around a gun is to edge your way
to the other side of it

my husband chose planes and gliders and rockets and any winged thing
he tested them, experiments, new inventions. machines he had once believed were such
gentle birds. how they fall out of the sky in wartime

he broke his back at least three times. he says he doesn't remember
the exact number of fractures, or which forty-three kilometre bicycle ride with which ribs
broken, which part of the spine. his right side entirely wrapped with strips of mattress ticking

the metal of the medal would not bend. I came downstairs because of the noise, he was
beating something in the fire with a poker. saying nothing. in what was left
of my grandmother's house.

why god made the winter so cold

what sick sense of humour was that? I am not an atheist, no, much simpler. I hate.

when there were no wools given for civilian clothes. no cottons even. running just barely a textile mill and ourselves in cellulose garbage *deutscher wald*

the soldiers younger and younger. with the rest of us shivering
through scenic forced lunchtime marches
all the workers round and round. the most amazing

propaganda. block up your ears you know none of it. the russians Our Soviet Friends until suddenly *untermenschen* like everyone else.

firebombs and firebirds. pretty matches.

wool would never have burned like that.

historic detail

towards the end you know they were rounding up young boys,
barely teenagers, if twelve is a teenager. their voices
not even broken. no guns, still in ragged youth
uniforms they were simply sent north and handed grenades, their
officer said:
pull out the pin and throw it as far as you can towards the russians

what, I heard a woman say in the Eger railway station, *are you just*
too lazy to shoot the boys yourself? that's what I heard
as she pulled out the pin and held time in her hand.

paper trails

you wrap the yarn around what's called a cop. it's a paper tube.
you can wrap other things around the cop first. if you like
you can wrap the cop in paper currency and then wrap
the yarn around this paper. it is all paper. then you must
write a letter to your former business associates in london, you
tell them there are certain tubes leaking water, ask advice,
you tell them a yarn, you list certain numbers
which relate to cops and paper, you admire your inventive
discretion. your necessary
invention.

you find a way to get out of your country. it is all about placing
paper in the right hands. it is about avoiding certain officers,
later on you will call them cops, you like the slang. you spend
several years without papers, saved by the layer of paper
previously wrapped around a cop,
hidden in the yarn.

am I only remembering it because my husband told me

And the money?
Wrapped under thread.
We shall go to england ho, to bonny bonny england

I hated england. it was so deeply
unoriginal & so terribly pleased with itself.
so rich that day-old bread was tossed out for the pigeons.

imagine feeding pigeons with bread a man might eat. that's what
rich countries do

there was a joke from Berlin, you must imagine it in their bitter
accent. while the Allies ate rats, they said, we here yah cook
Erzazt-Ratten,
not even real rats they gave us

it is a joke that translates poorly. I mean: we had eaten the rats
long ago, poor things.
or
we had become them

people are mislaid in this story. try to imagine the world then.
how big it seemed, how easy
to be trapped within it. how many borders to the maps set into
our mental scape. I was so sudden in england

I was surprised to see the rats were safe & sound.

I didn't know where my brother was. he was misplaced, he was
behind
some sort of curtain.

we lived at the top of the house & did not get along neither at first nor by the end of it

the leaving I carried in my mouth like a needle.
I sewed the story together, made it tight, with the seams pulled in,
nothing of the self leaked out. revenge is important like glue. we
went to england.
there are places you go to with no papers. I told my son no.
he was not to speak until he learned to say yes in english.
I taught him myself in that house where everyone hated us, four
families in one house, every morning I would lock my son and I,
just us two in our top floor bedroom, with a bottle of gin,
I taught christoph english until his name
was christopher and the gin had run out.

it's complicated, I used to be like everyone

but more than one language was what we needed in those days.

in england they said don't swear in French, don't cough in
german, they'll find you out.
don't stub your toe in any dialect. I acquired a new coarse
vocabulary.

smoking dried rose petals. dandelion leaves. rosemary. dreaming,
yes, dreaming of real tobacco.

and you mustn't go out of the house or past the edge of the
garden. no wonder we were

looking to go absolutely anywhere as long as it wasn't to remain,
england, spit on the ground.

the boiled sweets & hard metal teeth of the russians

(dreaming in england)

it is Prague and sub-zero and where is my old rat coat

tea in a glass, silver holder, a spoonful of raspberry jam
it will cure everything

this country is so inward, says the englishman, waving towards the
window of the Hotel Europa. we are close to the railway station
looking out on the good king's plaza, which is only
a street.

this country, he says

—but I have abandoned my efforts at listening. how many stories
must I really recall. my father and uncles sitting at small
round tables out on the Platz, small square pastries on
saucers, pale pink, pale yellow, hard icing

the café of the Hotel Europa is not quite right in my dream, the
colours are wrong,
and so what if I am
looking inward. map all these details there, on the inside
of my eyes.

displaced persons

you go on a journey or a stranger comes to town: these
are the only two stories. I am a stranger. I have gone on a journey.
how would you like me to tell the story?

society prefers us to have
a single & fixed address. the mail must reach us. the taxman will
know
where to collect. the mortician can take us away.

in Scotland they build special doors for the dead. to take the body
out of the house.

surely one can call oneself a traveller
even if the itinerary is not something selected in advance
from a colour brochure.

inter-continental

thank god I'd have loved any country after england, I fall deeply
for every new landscape, each
is a fine escape from that damn country. we got a telegram. short
and to the point

Wilhelm - alive - cuba - heading - for
- toronto - where

- the - hell

- are - you

full stop. I'd have packed my bags right then in less
than two hours,
my son in his clean shoes and shorts
my husband thinking Canada sounded rational, a different
20th century

my accent gone strange

we ended up there in the north, the west, the americas, it was
Wilhelm, we
could pin everything on that telegram, that telegram, he was alive
and
where the hell

wearing jewelry while in transit

a diamond bracelet sewn into the hem of a skirt
gives the fabric a heft that translates well into local currency

I have a good ear for languages

(use silk thread, it is thinner. more stitches
to hold your inheritance in place)

we have always been merchants and experts
in exchange

who doesn't have a past someone
will pay money for.

my thirtieth birthday

I have dressed as a man and prayed in a mosque in Bakhtaran
I have learned the Latin names of several yellow flowers
I have given birth to a son, and I did not drown him.

I have read novels in any one of four languages,
none of them written in Czech.
I have collected many pieces of Inuktituk sculpture.

I have worn second-hand shoes, the last pair in 1953. I have
learned to cook; have dieted three times,
have swum a four-mile race; and have left my home forever
by squeezing through a hole in the back fence.

I have forced myself to develop
a taste for jazz music. and I have once drunk a bottle
of Shalimar perfume because there was nothing else.
It did not make me so sick

as I had expected.

fortress

patio or teahouse or cave
window and ceiling and skyscraper, palace
and arcade, dome or cloister, cast iron
courtyard, stone balcony, rooftop:

the view as one stands at its edge.

I fall in love

with houses. the people within
secondary, just
temptations inside
the real delight of walls

people
are so much less reliable

I travelled looking for a home, I made
the itinerary into a house for myself

I was at ease en route

kurtz und gutes (Canadian winter)

I like the taste of water in this country. you can taste
how young it is, how it has never been drunk
before. (haven't you ever felt like that, as if you are about to be
drunk for the first time?)

how to recapture such virginity

the snow blows against the west side of the house, wind coming
off the lake, I climbed out the winter, I mean, the window,

waist-deep in the snowbank
I was in diamond-patterned pyjamas

a certain amount of ranting

full moon, it had been snowing for a week, solid, and finally
during the night it stopped, the temperature dropping, the snow
drifts froze. crystalline. I must have woken him up, some strange
sound from outside. moonlight tantalizing the room. I imagine
him groping out of bed and into slippers, slow walk down

to the living room. on the wrong side of the sliding doors there I
am, his wife, in pyjamas,
leaning my back to the glass. I can see from his face what he
expects, let's be honest, he doesn't
expect very much.

but he gets the door unlocked, he is surprised to see that what I'm
doing
in fact
is laughing. tears have iced in the corners of my eyes

my pyjamas are clotted snow, melting off me onto the rug

the gas fireplace turns on with a switch

my husband finds himself in the kitchen making coffee, instant,
mine black. his with three spoons of sugar. in front of the fireplace
I take the proffered cup
unsteadily from his hand,
sure sign that I haven't had a drink. I can see he is recalculating,
his estimates
wrong again.

difference

how a mind works, mine

to be passionately
alive yes, all the senses refuting common sense and plunging
deeply deeply

while he searched for knowledge. facts.

tempting to rely on such firm ground but
(even now you can feel it turning)

history is an earthquake (I said to him)
we were born on a fault line

some of us dancing

it is a type of paranoia.
do you really think such a sensation is not justified?

here, I'll open the cabinet where I keep them like butterflies. the
blue Canadian one. a crest, some processed paper. here the red
of the temporary one. look, the photo is at the back.
here is the pink and blue identity card. here a work permit. and
nowhere
is that grey
folded card. blank-faced. for remembrance. for forgetting.

do I make it sound hopeless? just because a nationality isn't
to be trusted, doesn't mean
you can't balance on the edge of the stage, arms outstretched:

I mean, I was smiling through my lipstick. I was smoking a
borrowed cigarette

ex-patriate

there is a town in what is now a Republic and everything
spirals from
that one tiny place, as if
it were the centre of the universe,

and it isn't. everyone wants
a place on which
to plant a flag, I am here and these are my colours,
but I have never been able to decide
on the pattern for the flag. whether
there should be loud zigzags
indicating my many travels, or should
there simply be a blank space or

and I think this is my favourite choice

could there be
a single die from a pair
of red plastic dice
I used to carry, which rolled unevenly
and always fell to five
or three

what would you choose
for your pirate ship sailing
from port to port, same baggage, always

thinking   Here is the homeland
I will want to hold on to. how "exiled"
rhymes with "escapee"
in another language,

not this one.

Wilhelm had a preference for unlikely farms.

walnuts. christmas trees.

he visited the flower farms of India, fields filled, fields of flowers,

yellow, blue, gold, green, rose,

the women, children, picking, develop diseases only ever seen
in flower-pickers.

he passed the farms on a train. the tea had a film of dust
across its surface.

the flower-pickers' lungs turn pastel-coloured with pollen dust,
their fingers callus, wearing out the fingerprint petal after petal.

he pressed a finger to his wrist, pulse counted.
does it hurt there? he said to himself. does it hurt—
there?

once a year I took a trip

any excuse, packing a bag, ticket in hand, the assigned
airline seat, a clean slate. my back to Canada.

the name on a passport is nothing. you can turn those letters into
anything you like.

especially if you are travelling towards a trusted companion, one
who recognizes you
whatever the costume.

yes, my son in school, and my husband's work face, and packing.
against my skin, airline tickets my semi-precious gems, Wilhelm
knew the colours I'd be
most smitten by. I'd meet him anywhere. that much was clear.

it was in Paris, I bought Josephine Baker's old shoes

narrow gold boots with white spat-style buttoning
small pointed toes & slight heel, the soles unused but the sides of
the boot showed how she walked, scuffing her arches together,
each footstep reassuring the next.

it was in a curiosity shop of the kind my brother adores: soldier
trunks from Napoleon's
russian failure, statuary stolen from graveyards. jewelry of the
deceased & painfully present. how it is our objects survive us, not
our art.

personally I have no interest in such places. that sort of surgery
—why peel the self apart? what
spills out is such peculiar detritus. yet

the shoes, displayed to show off the new & unworn soles.
stupid fool, who took the mark of the street
off Baker's shoes, as if she of all dancers
didn't touch the ground.

I never saw her perform, I was too young, & then,

a dancer is only a dancer so long as she is moving. shoes looking
as if she only stood
still for a portrait, yes she invented
herself a lady, white buttons up from toe along the ankle, her skin
beneath the kid

these shoes are as Glenn Gould's gloves

Wilhelm mutters to himself, setting out the money,
while the *antiquaire* wraps my purchase

a type of bread which is the taste of homesickness

dry dense white bread that isn't in fact white but more the colour
of melted butter. also there are raisins. I used to eat such bread
sitting on the church steps. waiting for my mother to come out
from visiting
the statue inside that she called hers.

bread that was the taste of spring, that time of year

I haven't ever seen the right type of bread elsewhere, I can't say
I haven't looked

I find other breads, equally good but not the one I am looking
for. I say it doesn't matter.
those places that aren't my home, I have no sickness, I am well
and homeless. I have had
the fine luxury of choosing my state

I live in a very good house beside a lake.
there are mountains, small ones, in the distance which I like to
look at.

don't talk to me of bread. I am old enough. I have no need of it.

speed

I too made some few experiments with
the engines, my husband said, suddenly cheerful, the waiter
bringing him a new steak,
acceptable finally. and while he talked and made
the others laugh, I remembered him then
as the daredevil I had married, the one who volunteered
to try out machines that specialized only
in falling from the air. he fell so many times he said
it didn't bother him

he describes with delight
the bastard skidoo he built one winter, years later on the Lake of
Two Mountains, it was an old jet engine and to it he strapped
a seat and set of skis. it was
precarious, to be generous, but he was ecstatic,

It Went Like Hell, he says, spreading Dijon mustard on the blood-
red steak. *the trick*
was to keep moving. if you hit a patch of thin ice slowly, well,
too bad.

but I am thinking of how I used to wake
in that house where bungalow-style we had each our own floor
to trace our nightmares on. how alone I would hear him get up,
his purposeful walk downstairs
through the dark, to where in his workroom
he could visit the machines he considered friends

the best part of courage

I have a great deal
of resentment. it isn't a fair complaint. I am after all
a lucky one. I have been alive all this time, I have the luxury
of looking at my son's classmates as they graduate this afternoon
in a stuffy gymnasium in safe brown Ontario.

I have always looked
upon the torn portion of the ticket. the part no longer
in my pocket. I roll the lint into a ball and consider it
the colour of the ground here in spring. it is May,

too late for the boys years ago. of Wilhelm's friends—two sons of
the nearest neighbour. their classmate at textile college a
Hungarian Jew who once beat
Wilhelm, blackening his eye quite deservedly. and
a glove manufacturer's son with fat white hands.
the professor hacked to death, a case of mistaken identity. three
of the others
dead as soldiers and one, dead in camp. Wilhelm only surviving.
up to a certain date.
there's no such thing
as dying well, I think.

but now, these boys, how different? are praised for their abilities
in sports and history and chemistry. their valedictorian emphasizes
Courage and
The Future. I look at the girders in the roof of the gym,
bad fairy at the christening.

my wish for you
is that you have the wit to run away.

courage is not what they say.

dark

what are you most afraid of?
we were
in the dark. it was night. I suppose
that's redundant.

I said: dying of course.

but we're all going to die, Wilhelm said, nothing can be done
about that. what else?

and I saw in the dark
that I would have to be honest, there would be nothing
he could do about that, either.
being without resources, I said. there are some things which
soothe
more reliably than cotton. people are a far lesser thing to be
depended upon.

but the resource of yourself, he said, you would be
surprised.

but I know I would not be. I pretended then
to sleep, there on the far side of the tent.

the money I keep in the bandage box

I am often puzzled by my husband's great reliance
on banks. but I don't argue with him. I think he too
has something up his sleeve in case of trouble

a man who can be relied upon to bicycle with a broken back,
is unlikely to be stymied by mere inflation.

he asked my brother once: what will you do if you become richer?
what's the point?
aren't you rich enough? think how much faster
it all disappears when there's too much of it.

it's healthier, this attitude of a working man. he has made
his money, and lost it, and made it again, on his name. it's
different for aristocrats,
he told me one night, you believe in rules. you don't
know any better.

keeping accounts

the aeroplane taxis on the runway, rolling smoothly into air
buoyed up by our expectations, the act of running away

I pack my carryon with what's necessary. so little is.

I have no fear of flying. my debts are paid: my cousin and his
family, never found in that small plane.
and there is the twice-broken back of my husband, he who truly
cannot remember how often the planes he tested
crashed.

it's not the falling, he told me once. those heady days when we
spoke
with the cushion of simile. he said, no it's the waiting that's bad,
waiting inside that falling silence for the sudden stop. it's long
as a lifetime

flying over China

what there is to like about other places
is the possible. an education in topography
just looking out the window. flying over all this,
Wilhelm said, staring out
the window of the plane: the size of things, it exhausts
our thin morals.

Sleeping Beauty

Chairman Mao has been unstuffed and buried now I hope. in the
ground, does a pickled body decay, when it's been admired
by so many for so many
years?

his head rested on the red velour pillow
a cushion more suited
to a white fluffy cat
than to a chairman in a grey-blue suit. his skin
especially at the temples, and also his ears,
rather uneasy to look at. the flag with five-point stars enormous
over his groin

a glass and pink granite coffin. no time for fairy tales, I hovered
there
only for an instant. sleeping beauty,
do all of us imagine his chest
to move, or only me as I turned and followed
the line away from him?

a personal history of Peru

I like that about South America: its complications are
—is it wrong to say, familiar? I feel
comfortable manoeuvring through such things. I sat reading, I
had attempted,
futile idea, on my return from Peru, to interest my neighbours

in a reading circle. we would meet
once a month to discuss a book. the book of the month.

I bought sixteen copies of this history of Peru but no one was
interested.

they prefer pretty baubles, fiction that glitters like candy
when it is sticky wet, when you have spit it from your mouth
because
it is too sweet, your teeth burning at the touch
of all those shining colours

I won't be able to explain, it's not so simple. the shelf beside my
bed loaded with copies of Peru, a reproach of private ritual.

pointing out

my husband lost a finger by the Lake. part of the index, he hadn't
been big on pointing anyhow. building the house
there, a moment of attention for the wrong detail, a sudden slip,
the round notched wheel in the chainsaw. he drove
holding his left hand
level with his ear, pleased with the automatic transmission in his
new blue lincoln
trying to keep his blood
off the upholstery. at hospital admissions he signed the form
as a doctor asked him Where is it?

Where's What? (Vhere's Vhat, he never did
get those double-you's sorted out, his laurence velk
standby, both official languages turned arch)

The Finger, the doctor waved his own hands,
should've brought her in, thrown some ice on her, we could've
hooked you back together. but as it is...

the scar finishes the finger tidily, a single knuckle,
and the next refrigerator we bought
had one of those ice makers
in the door. it made him laugh to demonstrate
the machinery, using his left hand, always, and then
when he'd notice the person looking he'd say, This Time
I've got Advance Planning. leaving the person beside him
confused, unclear in front of the avocado-coloured
refrigerator. his best metaphor.

William Tell

the restaurant had something resembling
table service. I held out my hand to a waiter who dutifully nodded
and ignored my desires. I was in that kind of mood, no harm in
being given
extra moments to contemplate
the salt thrown on the street outside and tracked
inside by my boots, however elegant. a colour in the rug picked at
my toes through their already-scarred leather. I should never have
told him my plan
to drown the baby in the toilet if she were a girl. of course he
would not understand, and who knows perhaps I would have.

go ahead, tell me a woman is just as good, can do
everything that a
—go on, tell me.

the waiter doesn't bring me a drink or a menu
until my son comes in from the Montreal night,
shaking snow from the collar of his coat. like
me, his shuttered face.

if I'd been born a man? all the right qualifications
for nothing. I'd have made a good
assassin. this
I do not say. no, instead I open the menu, consider
its opportunities. I am studying discretion
at much too late an age.

the reason I didn't get a room with a balcony

haven't you ever been in a taxi, the back passenger seat,
your door unlocked, driving down a highway thinking
if I open the door now...what about now, I think we're going fast enough
I wouldn't feel any

but that's the harm in it, I want to feel something, then
I lock the door, that gesture of the hopeless.

Avro Cadet G-ACHN, two-seater bi-winged, propeller in front

an unlikely slip of a thing I never believed in

believe is not *fly,* my husband said

but if not belief, then what keeps everyone aloft, every one of us?

the dust you eat

gold eaters, Sea of Marmara, Haghia Sophia

mosaics crumble to eye-level disappearance, saints and geometrics
dissolving: the eaters
crawl to church on their knees

scratch off a single glass square of gold and put it on your tongue.
swallow

devotion:

the mosaic slowly eaten by desire, by wanting

(bread can be transformed into flesh, and gold?)

a piece of the true church. the way it cuts in the throat and then
lodges
somewhere below the heart. swallow a piece of god—and does the
world change

I have been to Nishapur, Iranian city, where the ground itself
was exported: magical, edible earth, where poor women still eat
dirt. the clay fiends, addicted.

it is said
you can die of it.

the love affair as work of art

Istanbul: an affair of the heart, the old city made me dream
of Vienna again, what is it? the river? nothing to do with anything,
said Wilhelm, displeased, when I telephone him too early
forgetting
the hour's time change. easy for him, he lives on the edge
of what Vienna is now. his address
strictly present tense

my single bed with wooden trellised headboard, painted green and
red and faded,
the shuttered window keeping none of the street noise
from my sleep, I thought I—

this old dream of Vienna, something
about the colour of the buildings here, or it's
the ruined idea of an empire,
what it leaves behind when it's gone

Lord Byron's room

and Lady Montagu's, the first Englishwoman to inoculate
her children against smallpox, a fashion she learned
in Turkey, of course it was not Turkey then

take a bit of poison to protect yourself from what comes later

all velvet drapes now forgotten, and Lord Byron's monkey

limping down the hall, I have sprained my ankle twice, the same
ankle, and once broken my arm but that was skiing and hardly
counts

in Venice I believe in all that literature. everywhere else the world
inclines me
more towards non-fiction, I suppose you think what I mean

is television

boating

Venice is the city you go to before dying, Wilhelm said.
have you something up your sleeve? I asked, while
we stayed in the usual hotel.
Don Juan was written there, on the second floor

the curtains made me think of drowning in slow-motion. this city
is expert in wading out, into oblivion.

he was having trouble with stairs but not mentioning.
two canes

we spent a lot of time sitting down. coffee-houses, restaurants,
casinos. there's no loss of dignity being helped laborious
from the vaporetti. no gondolas. simply for tourists who pretend
romance

we stayed a month. it was not a carnival. he was always
so thirsty for beauty. he reread Thomas Mann, he used to cry
over novels. I reread the history
of Peru and held my tongue. one morning he said,
look at the sun. to hell with this. I hear Uganda's
really hopping these days

when you are too old for them to see where you've been

for no one remembers the language you speak & when you wake
in the night there is the
night nurse dispenser of medicines, giver of forgetting. you don't
want
to forget

lean my cheek against yours. no trace on your face to recall our
politics or cheekbones
both inherited from our whalebone grandmother. no witty
repartee, nothing to engineer
beyond the fork from plate to mouth. hand
trembling. we listen to *Lady*
in the Dark, old Weill recording in a cheap tape player, the
darkened
residence room. music's code; the soda counter
where Weill died sudden-like
in New York City. *I think maybe*
he had it easy, you say. *this room is so goddamn ugly*

you loved living in New York, you loved the american slang, you
loved

afterwards I sit under the hairdryer at the coiffeur,
keeping my hair brown, my lips red, my hands steady to translate
yours. can't I give these memories away, can't I put them
in a safe-deposit box & give the key to somebody else

how we'd rather be in the tropics. the trips you made through
Uganda, that last one, the earth beneath your feet is about to shift
you over, a cane in each hand

once upon a time I said don't worry I'll push the wheelchair. &
really
I thought
it was the truth

and it does

when he was dying again

the hospital room the most unpleasant shade

of green

my god couldn't there be a better colour

and it's so slow

this could take years

not waving

don’t think the drink was always
for forgetting, no there were mornings when it was for remember

don’t forget who you are, my mother preferred this cliché
to all others. her legacy such that I have never been able to

how fortunate, those who can change such a thing. throw
the papers, shredded, over the side,
as the ferry moves closer to Argentina.

another drink will cure the thing
even if it’s three days in the making, more bottles than
I’d like to accumulate
staggered through the apartment,

something about the view, in the rain
you know how everything smeared looks familiar
as if it might be somewhere else

three characters, one dead

tonight
I will dress up in the blue djellaba and speak with my face hidden
by the dark shadow of the hood, the rough fabric will keep me
warm against the night, the embroidery
will carry my soul
to heaven. leave my lies sitting still on the floor of Wilhelm's tiny
flat, a home which belongs to no one with him dead.
what's the point of that for a man like Wilhelm.
being dead doesn't suit him at all

I have some olives in a tin, the dry salt taste of them.
wrinkled skin and black, with the pits in of course. God,
american habits, taking the core
out of everything so as to stuff it with money.
take a few of these olives
they're bitter, best with a glass of imperfect
red wine, pour yourself as much as you like, while I tell you

in this story,
there is Wilhelm, a cane in his hand but still quite good on
his feet, he would dance
leaning a little heavily on his partner's arm but his steps were
impeccable. the second character is me, well-made-up, in good
jewelry, at forty
looking better than I did twenty years before.
this was due to a change in the light, I believe. and I had learned
to laugh, though one shouldn't believe
that sound, it is a trick that can be taught to anyone

the third character is not a person at all.
it is a place, the absence of such.
the third character in the story is the one
we were both searching for. my story is a detective novel,
it can be told
on an aeroplane or in a train compartment, as if we are hurtling
through a tunnel and
neither of us knows what is on the other side. when we emerge,

(push away this blue hood) I don't know what will be there. I will
have to finish the story. was I really there? can one of you
tell me what happened next?

this wilderness waiting for me all along

I would be happy
stopping here, a shift from early Sinatra to pre-Vegas melancholy,
in the wee small hours when
we were on a cruise boat, all those nine storeys out of the water.
my husband
standing on deck. how many stories did we cobble together to be there? waiting for the icebergs
to parade past, my husband and the ice.

oh he is on the side of the survivors, the ones who like living and do what they do
and are still here, while the landscape passes by.

why did we expect heroes? naked fools clutching swords. we are strange furry animals
swallowing our tails. my mouth still numb from a dentist's anaesthetic
even as the boat clears the Lion's Gate Bridge. heading to Alaska, a new bridge
constructed within my jaws. postcards as yet unwritten.

would it be better to say

I lied or, I am sorry?

would it be better
not to know? whether yes I felt the drowning surge forward, I
tried to surface
struggled for breath, or

no, the water was what I drank down like every drink
I had ever held in my hand

I used to think knowing
mattered, that fact and fiction both
could at least frame what went on, though not explain

and now I see that possibly
all those spoken words, all those written ones just add
to the confusion, and when I sank
for that moment before floating, what was it? silent?

the Republic and Pointe Claire

for years I thought
he was a thoughtless man

and then a few years too late for you and I, this impossible
possible future occurred, and the man
with the strange name was suddenly able
to return to the country that had been his,
or ours. and his decision
not to. his name is strange there too, now

I mean,
he visited. he drove all those roads that
he had unwillingly marched from and he looked
at landscape that
didn't seem right to his unnostalgic eyes

he took some photographs
and he came back to Pointe Claire
with the films in his carryon luggage

the past passes. it is invisible.
it is usually raining
just a little. it is not a thing to be retraced:

a lover might touch the palm of your hand
making one letter after another. no. it is past

and he likes
the cool month of September on the lake

the maples turn their leaves in the wind

Saint Émilion

I am now my own instrument
my own wheel of fortune

it is a type
of connoisseurship, to know the self
as some understand wine

it's all in the palate, how you roll
the taste of your life
around in your mouth. do you
spit it out?

Lisa Pasold is a freelance journalist who writes about travel, architecture and culture. She's been thrown off a train in Belarus, been fed the world's best pigeon pie in Marrakech, has taken the wrong bus in Bohemia, mushed huskies in the Yukon, and been cheated in the Venetian gambling halls of Ca' Vendramin Calergi. Her favourite game is roulette. She grew up in Montreal and currently lives in Paris. In 2003, her poetry appeared in *100 Poets Against the War* and *The Short Fuse Anthology.*